by Iain Gray

Lang**Syne**

PUBLISHING

WRITING *to* REMEMBER

Lang**Syne**

PUBLISHING

WRITING *to* REMEMBER

79 Main Street, Newtongrange,
Midlothian EH22 4NA
Tel: 0131 344 0414   Fax: 0845 075 6085
E-mail: info@lang-syne.co.uk
www.langsyneshop.co.uk

Design by Dorothy Meikle
Printed by Ricoh Print Scotland
© Lang Syne Publishers Ltd 2014

ISBN 978-1-85217-405-7

Higgins

MOTTO:
For one's country.

CREST:
A griffin clutching a sword.

NAME variations include:
Higgans
Higgens
Higgin
Higginson
O'Higgin
O'Higgins
Ó hAodhagain *(Gaelic)*
Ó hUigínn *(Gaelic)*

Chapter one:

Origins of Irish surnames

**According to an old saying, there are two types of Irish –
those who actually are Irish and those who wish they were.**

This sentiment is only one example of the allure that the
high romance and drama of the proud nation's history holds
for thousands of people scattered across the world today.

It's a sad fact, however, that the vast majority of Irish
surnames are found far beyond Irish shores, rather than on
the Emerald Isle itself.

The population stood at around eight million souls in
1841, but today it stands at fewer than six million.

This is mainly a tragic consequence of the potato
famine, also known as the Great Hunger, which devastated
Ireland between 1845 and 1849.

The Irish peasantry had become almost wholly reliant
for basic sustenance on the potato, first introduced from the
Americas in the seventeenth century.

When the crop was hit by a blight, at least 800,000
people starved to death while an estimated two million
others were forced to seek a new life far from their native
shores – particularly in America, Canada, and Australia.

The effects of the potato blight continued until about
1851, by which time a firm pattern of emigration had
become established.

Ireland's loss, however, was to the gain of the countries in which the immigrants settled, contributing enormously, as their descendants do today, to the well being of the nations in which their forefathers settled.

But those who were forced through dire circumstance to establish a new life in foreign parts never forgot their roots, or the proud heritage and traditions of the land that gave them birth.

Nor do their descendants.

It is a heritage that is inextricably bound up in the colourful variety of Irish names themselves – and the origin and history of these names forms an integral part of the vibrant drama that is the nation's history, one of both glorious fortune and tragic misfortune.

This history is well documented, and one of the most important and fascinating of the earliest sources are *The Annals of the Four Masters*, compiled between 1632 and 1636 by four friars at the Franciscan Monastery in County Donegal.

Compiled from earlier sources, and purporting to go back to the Biblical Deluge, much of the material takes in the mythological origins and history of Ireland and the Irish.

This includes tales of successive waves of invaders and settlers such as the Fomorians, the Partholonians, the Nemedians, the Fir Bolgs, the Tuatha De Danann, and the Laigain.

Of particular interest are the *Milesian Genealogies*,

because the majority of Irish clans today claim a descent from either Heremon, Ir, or Heber – three of the sons of Milesius, a king of what is now modern day Spain.

These sons invaded Ireland in the second millennium B.C, apparently in fulfilment of a mysterious prophecy received by their father.

This Milesian lineage is said to have ruled Ireland for nearly 3,000 years, until the island came under the sway of England's King Henry II in 1171 following what is known as the Cambro-Norman invasion.

This is an important date not only in Irish history in general, but for the effect the invasion subsequently had for Irish surnames.

'Cambro' comes from the Welsh, and 'Cambro-Norman' describes those Welsh knights of Norman origin who invaded Ireland.

But they were invaders who stayed, inter-marrying with the native Irish population and founding their own proud dynasties that bore Cambro-Norman names such as Archer, Barbour, Brannagh, Fitzgerald, Fitzgibbon, Fleming, Joyce, Plunkett, and Walsh – to name only a few.

These 'Cambro-Norman' surnames that still flourish throughout the world today form one of the three main categories in which Irish names can be placed – those of Gaelic-Irish, Cambro-Norman, and Anglo-Irish.

Previous to the Cambro-Norman invasion of the twelfth century, and throughout the earlier invasions and settlement of those wild bands of sea rovers known as the Vikings in the eighth and ninth centuries, the population of the island was relatively small, and it was normal for a person to be identified through the use of only a forename.

But as population gradually increased and there were many more people with the same forename, surnames were adopted to distinguish one person, or one community, from another.

Individuals identified themselves with their own particular tribe, or 'tuath', and this tribe – that also became known as a clann, or clan – took its name from some distinguished ancestor who had founded the clan.

The Gaelic-Irish form of the name Kelly, for example, is Ó Ceallaigh, or O'Kelly, indicating descent from an original 'Ceallaigh', with the 'O' denoting 'grandson of.' The name was later anglicised to Kelly.

The prefix 'Mac' or 'Mc', meanwhile, as with the clans of the Scottish Highlands, denotes 'son of.'

Although the Irish clans had much in common with their Scottish counterparts, one important difference lies in what are known as 'septs', or branches, of the clan.

Septs of Scottish clans were groups who often bore an entirely different name from the clan name but were under the clan's protection.

In Ireland, septs were groups that shared the same name and who could be found scattered throughout the four provinces of Ulster, Leinster, Munster, and Connacht.

The 'golden age' of the Gaelic-Irish clans, infused as their veins were with the blood of Celts, pre-dates the Viking invasions of the eighth and ninth centuries and the Norman invasion of the twelfth century, and the sacred heart of the country was the Hill of Tara, near the River Boyne, in County Meath.

Known in Gaelic as 'Teamhar na Rí', or Hill of Kings, it was the royal seat of the 'Ard Rí Éireann', or High King of Ireland, to whom the petty kings, or chieftains, from the island's provinces were ultimately subordinate.

It was on the Hill of Tara, beside a stone pillar known as the Irish 'Lia Fáil', or Stone of Destiny, that the High Kings were inaugurated and, according to legend, this stone would emit a piercing screech that could be heard all over Ireland when touched by the hand of the rightful king.

The Hill of Tara is today one of the island's main tourist attractions.

Opposition to English rule over Ireland, established in the wake of the Cambro-Norman invasion, broke out frequently and the harsh solution adopted by the powerful forces of the Crown was to forcibly evict the native Irish from their lands.

These lands were then granted to Protestant colonists, or 'planters', from Britain.

Many of these colonists, ironically, came from Scotland and were the descendants of the original 'Scotti', or 'Scots', who gave their name to Scotland after migrating there in the fifth century A.D., from the north of Ireland.

Colonisation entailed harsh penal laws being imposed on the majority of the native Irish population, stripping them practically of all of their rights.

The Crown's main bastion in Ireland was Dublin and its environs, known as the Pale, and it was the dispossessed peasantry who lived outside this Pale, desperately striving to eke out a meagre living.

It was this that gave rise to the modern-day expression of someone or something being 'beyond the pale'.

Attempts were made to stamp out all aspects of the ancient Gaelic-Irish culture, to the extent that even to bear a Gaelic-Irish name was to invite discrimination.

This is why many Gaelic-Irish names were anglicised with, for example, and noted above, Ó Ceallaigh, or O'Kelly, being anglicised to Kelly.

Succeeding centuries have seen strong revivals of Gaelic-Irish consciousness, however, and this has led to many families reverting back to the original form of their name, while the language itself is frequently found on the fluent tongues of an estimated 90,000 to 145,000 of the island's population.

Ireland's turbulent history of religious and political strife is one that lasted well into the twentieth century, a landmark century that saw the partition of the island into the twenty-six counties of the independent Republic of

Ireland, or Eire, and the six counties of Northern Ireland, or Ulster.

Dublin, originally founded by Vikings, is now a vibrant and truly cosmopolitan city while the proud city of Belfast is one of the jewels in the crown of Ulster.

It was Saint Patrick who first brought the light of Christianity to Ireland in the fifth century A.D.

Interpretations of this Christian message have varied over the centuries, often leading to bitter sectarian conflict – but the many intricately sculpted Celtic Crosses found all over the island are symbolic of a unity that crosses the sectarian divide.

It is an image that fuses the 'old gods' of the Celts with Christianity.

All the signs from the early years of this new millennium indicate that sectarian strife may soon become a thing of the past – with the Irish and their many kinsfolk across the world, be they Protestant or Catholic, finding common purpose in the rich tapestry of their shared heritage.

Chapter two:
Hereditary poets

The origins of the Higgins name are as fascinating as the lives and times of its bearers, who over the centuries have made a significant contribution to the rich tapestry that is Ireland's history.

In England, 'Higgins' is derived from 'Hicke' or 'Dick', a nickname for the common name 'Richard', while the Irish Gaelic forms are Ó hUiggín and Ó hAodhagain.

The latter indicates 'descent from little Aodh', with 'Aodh' later anglicised as 'Hugh', while Aodh was an ancient pagan god of fire.

Ó hUiggín, meanwhile, is said to indicate 'descendant of Vikings', or 'seafarer', with 'uiggin' equivalent to the Norse word for 'Viking'.

This would imply a descent, at least for some bearers of the Higgins name, from those fierce Scandinavian sea rovers whose sinister longboats first appeared off Irish shores in the closing years of the eighth century A.D.

Raids continued along the coastline until they made their first forays inland in 836 A.D., while a year later a Viking fleet of 60 vessels sailed into the River Boyne.

By 841 A.D. the Vikings, or Ostmen as they were also known, had established a number of strongholds on the island, but their raids began to ease off before returning with a terrifying and bloody vengeance in about 914 A.D.

It was not until about 30 years later that the raids came to an end, by which time they had established permanent settlements in Ireland, particularly in Dublin and other coastal areas such as present day Waterford, Wexford, Carlingford and Strangford.

The common consensus, however, is that while some bearers of the Higgins name may indeed have Viking blood coursing through their veins, the vast majority trace a descent from a grandson of the celebrated late fourth century Niall Noíghiallach, better known as the great warrior king Niall of the Nine Hostages.

His grandson is said to have been named Uigín – although there is no indication as to exactly how this name was adopted many centuries before the arrival on Irish shores of the Vikings.

Niall of the Nine Hostages was the founder of what became the great Uí Néill ('descendants of Niall') dynasty of native Irish clans that were split into the Northern Uí Néill and the Southern Uí Néill.

Through Uigín, the ancestors of today's bearers of the Higgins name were members of a branch of the Southern Uí Néill known as Uí Cheallaigh, itself a sub-branch of the Cenél Fiachach.

Known collectively as the Muintir Uigín – 'People descended from Uigín' – they flourished for centuries with main seats at Kilbeg, in Co. Westmeath, and in Dooghorne, Monteige and Ballynary in Co. Sligo.

An O'Higgins Clan Association was officially registered with the independent authority, Clans of Ireland, in 2005 and a descendant of the Ballynary branch, Thomas O'Higgins, was recognised as Chief of the Clan.

Four years later, in 2009, James F. Higgins of Nebraska, in the United States, was appointed as Clan Poet, in recognition of an ancient Higgins tradition.

This was their honoured role for centuries as skilled poets – so skilled in the art that they served for centuries as hereditary poets to powerful clans that included the O'Neills, Maguires, O'Dohertys and MacDermots.

One indication of the high regard in which they were held as poets throughout the island comes from Sir James Terry, the Herald at the Court-in-Exile in France from 1690 to 1720 of King James II (James VII of Scotland).

Referring to them as the Muinter Uigínn, he described them as "most ancient, most noble and most illustrious" hereditary poets.

The role of poet could sometimes be one fraught with truly dire consequences, as the fate of the sixteenth century poet Taolhg Dall Ó hUigínn illustrates.

'Dall' is the Irish Gaelic for 'blind', but despite his affliction Taolhg, who lived from 1550 to 1595, composed hundreds of poems in his lifetime from his seat at Doogherne, in Co. Sligo.

He was a master of satire, and this proved to be his undoing when he died after having his tongue cut out by the powerful O'Haras in revenge for a vicious satire he had composed against them.

Also in Co. Sligo, Flaithbheartach was a famed Higgins poet of the early tenth century.

What ultimately proved to be the death knell of the ancient Gaelic Order of native Irish clans such as Ó hUigínn was sounded in the late twelfth century through the Norman invasion of the island and the subsequent consolidation of the power of the English Crown.

One indication of the harsh treatment meted out to them can be found in a desperate plea sent to Pope John XII by leading Irish chieftains in 1318.

They stated: 'As it very constantly happens, whenever an Englishman, by perfidy or craft, kills an Irishman, however noble, or however innocent, be he clergy or layman, there is no penalty or correction enforced against the person who may be guilty of such wicked murder.

'But rather the more eminent the person killed and the higher rank which he holds among his own people, so much more is the murderer honoured and rewarded by the English, and not merely by the people at large, but also by the religious and bishops of the English race.'

The plight of the native Irish further deteriorated through the policy of 'plantation', or settlement of loyal Protestants on their lands.

Started during the reign from 1491 to 1547 of Henry VIII, whose Reformation effectively outlawed the established Roman Catholic faith throughout his dominions, the policy of plantation continued during the subsequent reigns of Elizabeth I, James I (James VI of Scotland), and in the aftermath of the Cromwellian invasion of 1649.

Ordained a Roman Catholic priest in Spain in 1627, Peter Higgins later returned to his native Ireland and in the 1630s established a priory at Naas, in Co. Kildare.

In March of 1642, he was executed following an edict that all Catholic priests were to be killed, while 350 years later Pope John Paul II beatified him, along with 17 other Irish martyrs who had died for their faith.

Following the Nine Years War of 1641 to 1649 and the subsequent Cromwellian invasion and conquest of Ireland, many bearers of the Higgins name found themselves reduced to tenants on their own lands, while the Monteige branch of the clan in Co. Sligo had to relocate to Co. Limerick.

Many bearers of the name subsequently became exiles, not only making significant contributions to those lands in which they settled, but also achieving high honours and distinction.

Chapter three:

On foreign shores

A further dispersal of native Irish to foreign parts followed in the wake of what is known in Ireland as *Cogadh an Dá Rí*, or The War of the Two Kings.

This was sparked off in 1688 when the Stuart monarch James II (James VII of Scotland) was deposed and fled into exile in France.

The Protestant William of Orange and his wife were invited to take up the thrones of Scotland, Ireland and England – but James still had significant support in Ireland, with his supporters known as Jacobites.

A series of military encounters followed, culminating in James's defeat by an army commanded by William at the battle of the Boyne on July 12, 1690.

The Williamite forces later besieged Limerick and the Jacobites were forced into surrender in September of 1691.

A peace treaty, known as the Treaty of Limerick followed, under which those willing to swear an oath of loyalty to William were allowed to remain in their native land.

Those reluctant to do so, including many bearers of the Higgins name, were allowed to seek exile on foreign shores, where they joined the military services of France and Spain.

Among those who flocked to the Court-in-Exile of

James II in France was the family of John Higgins, who was born in Limerick in 1678.

But rather than entering military service in the famed Irish Brigades, he left for Spain in 1700 after studying medicine and qualifying as a physician.

Serving as a medical officer to what were then the combined Spanish and French military forces, by 1718 his medical skills were recognised through his appointment as president of the Royal Academy of Medicine and Surgery of Seville.

Later ennobled by Philip V of Spain as Councillor of Castille, he was also made a baronet and knight by James II's successor, James III, five years before his death in 1729.

Honoured to this day for their significant contributions to the development of the modern day nations of Peru and Chile, Ambrosio O'Higgins and his son Bernardo O'Higgins were of the Ballynary stock of the family.

Born in 1720, Ambrosia O'Higgins left his native Ireland for Spain in 1751 and worked for a time in a trading house before leaving five years later for what was then Spanish America.

It was while in the Spanish colony of La Plata, in Argentina that he put forward a proposal for the development of an overland route, over the Andes, between Argentina and Chile.

Appointed engineer and draughtsman to the Spanish

Imperial Service, he oversaw the daunting task, which was successfully completed by 1766.

Appointed a brigadier in the army of the imperial service, he later became Captain General and Governor of Chile and was honoured by Charles III of Spain with a baronetcy.

At the time of his death in 1801, he was Viceroy of Peru – which then was comprised of modern day Peru, Chile, Bolivia, parts of western Brazil and northwest Argentina.

Recognised today as one of Chile's founding fathers, Bernardo O'Higgins was his illegitimate son.

Born in 1778 in the Chilean city of Chillán, O'Higgins was of Irish descent through his father and of Basque descent through his father's mistress for many years, Isabel Riquelime.

Although not officially recognised by his father, he nevertheless paid for his education in England and bequeathed him some of his South American estates.

But a life of gentlemanly leisure on his estates was not for the bold Bernardo.

Inspired by the revolutionary ideals of America's struggle for independence from Britain, he fought with distinction as an army general at the side of José de San Martín for Chile's independence from Spain during the Chilean War of Independence.

With Chile freed from Spanish rule, he later served, from 1817 to 1823, as the second Supreme Director of Chile.

He died in 1842, and among his many memorials is the *Avenida Libertador General Bernardo O'Higgins*, the grand main thoroughfare of the Chilean capital of Santiago.

Back in the Higgins homeland of Ireland, several figures of the name have played important roles in politics.

Most notable of these was Kevin O'Higgins, who was born in 1892 in Stradbally, Co. Laois.

A prominent figure in the Irish War of Independence, he served as Minister for Justice in the Irish Free State that was formed in 1922.

But as a result of the bitter and bloody nationalist infighting that erupted shortly after the foundation of the Free State, Irish Republican gunmen assassinated him in July of 1927.

His brother, Thomas F. O'Higgins, was the senior Irish politician, who five years before his death in 1953, was appointed the Republic's Minister of Defence, while his sons Michael O'Higgins and Tom O'Higgins, also served in the Irish Parliament.

In Australia, Henry Bournes Higgins, commonly known as H.B. Higgins, born in 1851 in Co. Mayo, was the lawyer who rose to become a Justice of the High Court of Australia after immigrating there with his family at the age of 19; he died in 1929.

Also in the justiciary, Dame Rosalyn Higgins, born Rosalyn Cohen in London in 1937, at the time of writing has the distinction of being the first female judge to be elected to the International Court of Justice, a post in which she acted as president from 2006 to 2009.

Bearers of the Higgins name have also been highly successful entrepreneurs.

Born in 1863 in Sabine, Texas, Patillo Higgins was the American businessman instrumental in the discovery and exploitation of the Lone Star state's Spindletop oil field.

A self-taught geologist, and founder of the Higgins Standard Oil Company, Higgins, who died in 1955, was known as "the prophet of Spindletop" – which, by its second year of operation in 1902, was producing more than 17 million barrels of oil a year.

Recognised in having played a vital role in Allied victory during the Second World War, Andrew Jackson Higgins, better known as Andrew J. Higgins, was born in 1886 in Columbus, Nebraska.

As the founder and owner in the early 1930s of Higgins Industries, based in New Orleans, he was responsible for the development and manufacture of 'Higgins Boats' during the Second World War.

More famously known as LCVPs (Landing Craft, Vehicle, Personnel), they proved indispensable during the Allied landings on the beaches of Normandy in 1944 and during America's operations in the Pacific against the Japanese.

Even Hitler recognised the vital role that the LCVPs were playing, bitterly describing Higgins as "the new

Noah", while American General Dwight D. Eisenhower described him as "the man who won the war for us."

"If Higgins had not designed and built those LCVPs", Eisenhower said, "we never could have landed over an open beach. The whole strategy of the war would have been different."

In addition to the LCVPs, Higgins Industries also produced torpedo tubes, gun turrets, smoke generators and the motor torpedo boats known as PT Boats.

Higgins died seven years after the end of the conflict, and is honoured through the Andrew Jackson Higgins National Memorial in his native Columbus, while part of U.S. Route 81, near his hometown, is named the Andrew Jackson Higgins Expressway.

Chapter four:

On the world stage

Bearers of the Higgins name and its spelling variants have also gained distinction in a variety of other pursuits, ranging from sport and music to film and literature.

Known to snooker fans as "Hurricane" because of the speed of his play, **Alex Higgins** was the master of the game who was born in 1949 in Belfast.

Taking up snooker at the age of 11, it was nevertheless a career as a jockey that he had originally hoped for.

Leaving his native Northern Ireland at the age of only 14 for England to train as a jockey, he had to return only two years later because the weight he had gained ruled him out of competitive horse racing.

This was to prove to the benefit of Higgins in particular and the world of snooker in general, as he again picked up the snooker cue and went on to win a string of major championships.

By the age of 19 he had won both the Northern Ireland Snooker Championship and the All-Ireland Snooker Championship, while by the age of 22 he won his first World Snooker Championship.

A second World Championship title followed in 1982, while he was also the winner of the UK Championship title in 1978, took Masters titles in both 1978 and 1981, and partnered Jimmy White to win the 1984 World Doubles Championship.

Despite his often unpredictable and volatile nature, fans fondly knew him as 'the People's Champion', but his fast living lifestyle and gambling eventually took its toll.

Estimated to have earned, and spent, between £3m and £4m during his playing career, he was eventually reduced to playing for small amounts of cash at venues throughout Northern Ireland.

Diagnosed with throat cancer in 1998, he died in his native Belfast in July of 2010, three years after the publication of his autobiography *Hurricane: My Story*.

From Northern Ireland to Scotland, **John Higgins**, nicknamed "the Wizard of Wishaw", is the professional snooker player who was born in the Lanarkshire town in 1975.

The winner, at the time of writing, of 21 ranking titles, including the World Snooker Championship in 1998, 2007 and 2009, he turned professional at the age of 17.

In May of 2010, the World Professional Billiards and Snooker Association suspended Higgins, who was awarded an MBE in 2008 for his services to the sport, from tournament play pending investigation into newspaper claims that he had been involved in match fixing.

He was cleared of these allegations four months later.

Also on the snooker table, **Andrew Higginson**, born in

1977 in Cheshire, is the English professional player who reached the final of the Welsh Open Championship in 2007.

From snooker to golf, **David Higgins**, born in 1972 in Co. Cork, is the Irish professional golfer who, by the age of 21, was the Republic's leading amateur.

He won the Ulster PGA Championship in 1995, a year after turning professional, while to date he can also boast three Challenge Tour wins.

In American football, **Johnnie Lee Higgins**, born in 1983 in Sweeney, Texas, is the talented wide receiver who signed in 2007 for the Oakland Raiders of the National Football League.

In Australian Rules football, **Shaun Higgins**, born in 1988 in Victoria, plays for the Western Bulldogs in the Australian Football League.

From football to baseball, Michael Higgins was the third baseman in Major League better known by his nickname of **Pinky Higgins**.

Born in 1909 in Red Oak, Texas, he played for teams that include Philadelphia Athletics, Boston Red Sox and the Detroit Tigers from 1955 to 1965.

Before his death in 1969, he was also a baseball scout and manager.

The Autosport National Rally Driver of the Year in both 1997 and 2000, **Mark Higgins** is the British rally driver who was born in 1971 in the Isle of Man.

A regular competitor in the British Rally Championship,

he was also a stunt driver for the James Bond *Quantum of Solace* movie.

In the saddle, **Roy Higgins**, born in 1938 in Koondrook, Victoria, is the former Australian jockey who won the prestigious Melbourne Cup on *Light Fingers* in 1965 and on *Red Handed* two years later.

Awarded an MBE for his services to the sport, he is now a racing commentator for Australian radio and television.

Bearers of the Higgins name have also made their mark on the world of music.

In contemporary pop music, Melissa Higgins, born in 1983 in Melbourne and better known as **Missy Higgins**, is the Australian singer and songwriter whose hit singles include *Where I Stood and Scar* – which won the 2004 Australian Recording Industry Association Music Award for Best Pop Release.

Of Irish and Hungarian family roots, **The Higgins** are the Canadian three-piece country music group composed of the siblings John Higgins, born in 1982 in Vancouver, Eileen, born in 1986 and Kathleen, born in 1988.

The group's many awards include a 2008 Canadian Country Music award for Album of the Year and the 2008 award for Group of the Year.

Born in 1939 in Andover, Massachusetts, **Jon Higgins** was the American musician, teacher and scholar renowned for his skill in the field of Carnatic music – the music associated with the south of the Indian sub-continent.

A co-founder of the Indian music studies programme at Toronto's York University in 1971, he died in 1984.

In a different musical genre, **Billy Higgins** was the acclaimed American jazz drummer who was born in 1936.

Before his death in 2001, he had played and recorded with fellow jazz luminaries who included Ornette Coleman, Milt Jackson, Thelonius Monk and Art Pepper.

In 1989 he co-founded The World Stage in Los Angeles, a centre to promote young jazz musicians, while shortly before his death he appeared as a jazz drummer in the film *Southlander*.

Better known by his stage name of **Dieselboy**, Damian Higgins is the internationally acclaimed drum and bass musician, disc jockey and record producer who was born in 1972 in Tarpon Springs, Florida.

Born in 1834 in New York City, **Henry Lee Higginson** was the wealthy American businessman who used part of his fortune in 1881 to found what is now the world-renowned Boston Symphony Orchestra; he died in 1919.

In the creative world of art, **William Higgins** was the American painter who was born in 1884 in Shelbyville, Indiana.

After studying art at the Art Institute of Chicago and the Chicago Academy of Fine Arts, he later moved to Taos, in New Mexico, where in 1915 he joined the Taos Society of Artists.

He died in 1949, but his enduring legacy includes

paintings such as *Taos from the Hillside*, *The Blue Shawl* and *New Mexico Skies*.

In the sciences, **William Higgins**, born in 1763 in Collooney, Co. Sligo, and who died in 1825, was the visionary Irish chemist credited as one of the early proponents of atomic theory.

In the world of the written word, **Aidan Higgins**, born in 1927 in Celbridge, Co. Kildare, is the Irish writer whose first novel, the 1966 *Langrishe*, won the James Tait Black Memorial Prize for Fiction.

His other works include the 2005 *Windy Arbours* and, from 2010, *Darkling Plains: Texts for the Air*.

Also a lawyer, newspaper columnist and college professor, George Vincent Higgins, born in 1939 in Brockton, Massachusetts, and better known as **George V. Higgins**, was the American author best known for his series of best-selling crime novels that include his 1972 *The Friends of Eddie Coyle* and *At End of Day*.

He died in 1999.

Better known by his pseudonym of **Jack Higgins**, Harry Patterson is the best-selling thriller writer who was born in 1929 in Newcastle upon Tyne.

The author to date of more than 60 novels, it was his 1975 Second World War thriller *The Eagle has Landed* that first brought him to international attention.

The novel was adapted for film a year later, starring Michael Caine, while other best-sellers include the 1977

The Valhalla Exchange, his 1982 *Touch the Devil* and, from 1985, *Confessional*.

On the stage, **Terri Higginson**, born in 1969 in Burlington, Ontario is the Canadian film, television and theatre actress who won a 2000 Gemini Award for Best Performance by an Actress in a Leading Dramatic Role for her performance in *The City*.

Also the recipient of a 2004 Saturn Award for Best Supporting Actress for her role in the television series *Stargate Atlantis*, other films in which she has appeared include the 1991 *The Photographer's Wife* and the 2009 *Smile of April*.

On British television, **Huw Higginson**, born in 1964 in Hillingdon, Middlesex is the English actor best known for his role from 1989 to 1999 as police constable George Garfield in the police drama series *The Bill*.

One particularly intrepid and pioneering bearer of the Higgins name was the American journalist and author **Marguerite Higgins**, recognised today as having advanced the cause of equal access to war zones for female war correspondents.

Born in 1920 in Hong Kong, where her American father worked for a shipping company, she joined the staff of the *New York Herald Tribune* as a news reporter in 1942, eventually persuading its management to assign her to war-torn Europe.

It was in Germany in April of 1945 that she witnessed

the horror of the newly liberated Dachau concentration camp, later receiving a U.S. Army campaign ribbon for her assistance during the surrender of the camp's S.S. guards.

After covering the Nuremberg war crimes trials and the Soviet blockade of Berlin, she was appointed chief of the *Tribune's* Tokyo office in 1950, and, despite initial fierce opposition from some quarters, covered the Korean War.

Her coverage of the conflict resulted in her becoming the first woman to win a Pulitzer Prize, in 1951, for international reporting.

Her dogged persistence later led to her being granted interviews with the Spanish dictator Francisco Franco, the Soviet Union's Nikita Khrushchev and India's Jawaharlal Nehru, while in 1955 she became chief of the *Tribune's* Moscow bureau.

Leaving the *Tribune* for *Newsday* magazine in 1963, she later covered the Vietnam War and wrote a best-selling book about the conflict, *Our Vietnam Nightmare*.

She died in 1966 from a tropical disease that she had contracted on one of her many assignments, and as a mark of honour was interred in Washington's Arlington National Cemetery – also the final resting place of her husband, U.S. Air Force General William E. Hall, whom she had married in 1952.

Key dates in Ireland's history from the first settlers to the formation of the Irish Republic:

circa 7000 B.C.	Arrival and settlement of Stone Age people.
circa 3000 B.C.	Arrival of settlers of New Stone Age period.
circa 600 B.C.	First arrival of the Celts.
200 A.D.	Establishment of Hill of Tara, Co. Meath, as seat of the High Kings.
circa 432 A.D.	Christian mission of St. Patrick.
800-920 A.D.	Invasion and subsequent settlement of Vikings.
1002 A.D.	Brian Boru recognised as High King.
1014	Brian Boru killed at battle of Clontarf.
1169-1170	Cambro-Norman invasion of the island.
1171	Henry II claims Ireland for the English Crown.
1366	Statutes of Kilkenny ban marriage between native Irish and English.
1529-1536	England's Henry VIII embarks on religious Reformation.
1536	Earl of Kildare rebels against the Crown.
1541	Henry VIII declared King of Ireland.
1558	Accession to English throne of Elizabeth I.
1565	Battle of Affane.
1569-1573	First Desmond Rebellion.
1579-1583	Second Desmond Rebellion.
1594-1603	Nine Years War.
1606	Plantation' of Scottish and English settlers.
1607	Flight of the Earls.
1632-1636	Annals of the Four Masters compiled.
1641	Rebellion over policy of plantation and other grievances.
1649	Beginning of Cromwellian conquest.
1688	Flight into exile in France of Catholic Stuart monarch James II as Protestant Prince William of Orange invited to take throne of England along with his wife, Mary.
1689	William and Mary enthroned as joint monarchs; siege of Derry.
1690	Jacobite forces of James defeated by William at battle of the Boyne (July) and Dublin taken.

1691	Athlone taken by William; Jacobite defeats follow at Aughrim, Galway, and Limerick; conflict ends with Treaty of Limerick (October) and Irish officers allowed to leave for France.
1695	Penal laws introduced to restrict rights of Catholics; banishment of Catholic clergy.
1704	Laws introduced constricting rights of Catholics in landholding and public office.
1728	Franchise removed from Catholics.
1791	Foundation of United Irishmen republican movement.
1796	French invasion force lands in Bantry Bay.
1798	Defeat of Rising in Wexford and death of United Irishmen leaders Wolfe Tone and Lord Edward Fitzgerald.
1800	Act of Union between England and Ireland.
1803	Dublin Rising under Robert Emmet.
1829	Catholics allowed to sit in Parliament.
1845-1849	The Great Hunger: thousands starve to death as potato crop fails and thousands more emigrate.
1856	Phoenix Society founded.
1858	Irish Republican Brotherhood established.
1873	Foundation of Home Rule League.
1893	Foundation of Gaelic League.
1904	Foundation of Irish Reform Association.
1913	Dublin strikes and lockout.
1916	Easter Rising in Dublin and proclamation of an Irish Republic.
1917	Irish Parliament formed after Sinn Fein election victory.
1919-1921	War between Irish Republican Army and British Army.
1922	Irish Free State founded, while six northern counties remain part of United Kingdom as Northern Ireland, or Ulster; civil war up until 1923 between rival republican groups.
1949	Foundation of Irish Republic after all remaining constitutional links with Britain are severed.